PAISLEY
PEOPLE & PLACES

ELLEN FARMER
& THE OLD PAISLEY SOCIETY

SUTTON PUBLISHING

Sutton Publishing Limited
Phoenix Mill · Thrupp · Stroud
Gloucestershire · GL5 2BU

First published 2004

Title Page: Canal Street. The Paisley
Co-operative Manufacturing Society (PCMS)
owned many properties in the town. These
buildings were owned by the 'Co-op', as it
was affectionately known, but in the 1950s
this row was demolished to make way for
the development of modern houses with
better facilities. *(OPS)*

British Library Cataloguing in Publication Data
A catalogue record for this book is available from the
British Library.

ISBN 0-7509-3509-X

Typeset in 10.5/13.5 Photina.
Typesetting and origination by
Sutton Publishing Limited.
Printed and bound in England by
J.H. Haynes & Co. Ltd, Sparkford.

One of the entrances to Ferguslie House, home of a member of the Coats family, who owned
the large Ferguslie Mill complex, *c.* 1920. The house was not far from the mill. Standing in
the driveway are William Steel and his son, also called William. *(Isobel Steel)*

CONTENTS

The Barbour drinking fountain at the junction of Neilston Road and Calside, *c.* 1970. The fountain was donated by William Barbour for the benefit of the townspeople, at a time when there were fewer food or drink takeaways. William Barbour was also a patron of the local hospital and made many donations to its welfare. *(OPS)*

FOREWORD

BY DOUGLAS ALEXANDER MP

It is a great honour as the MP for Paisley South to be asked to write the foreword to *Paisley People & Places*, the follow-up to *A Century of Paisley*, Ellen Farmer's illuminating record of our town through the twentieth century.

Where *A Century of Paisley* gave us a glimpse of our town in an age of rapid scientific and industrial progress, *Paisley People & Places* takes a closer look at the lives of those who helped shape the Paisley we know today.

Scotland's largest town has a rich and colourful history. An industrial powerhouse in the nineteenth and twentieth centuries, it was home to some of the country's great industries, most notably, but not exclusively, weaving and textiles. Today, the distinctive Paisley Pattern – renowned across the world – remains a potent symbol of an industry that became a byword for quality and excellence.

Paisley's skyline is defined by the physical landmarks of its industrial past. One of the most striking, the Abbey Mill Centre, with its commanding chimney, is now

One of the Paisley Co-operative Manufacturing Society's stores, 1950s. This one seemed to sell everything from hardware to hosiery and included a hairdressing section. The history of the PCMS dates back to 1862, when a few Paisley weavers and several shopkeepers met to consider whether they could carry the principle of co-operative living into the manufacture of goods. The result was the formation of the Paisley Co-operative Manufacturing Society, which still operates today. A provisional committee of seven people was appointed to carry out the proposals. (*Maurice Irvine*)

home to a modern office complex and a new development is under way at the nearby former finishing mill. In Paisley, the past is helping to shape our shared future.

As traditional manufacturing industries gave way to more diverse employment through facilities like Paisley University, the Braehead complex and the nearby airport, so life has changed for the citizens of Paisley. Community spirit remains strong and the creative arts thrive, thanks largely to the work of organisations like PACE and the Paisley Arts Centre. Sporting interests have expanded. St Mirren FC still entertains thousands of loyal fans each week, but football is no longer the only game in town.

Today, Paisley is a modern, confident town, its people drawn from the four corners of the world. *Paisley People & Places* examines the contribution made by the sizeable immigrant community, the 'newcomers' who gave Paisley a more diverse and cosmopolitan face, from the Highland crofters and farmers lured by the promise of work in the new industries, to the Italian migrants who inspired a culinary revolution.

Ours is a town that also boasts some fine examples of Scottish architecture, from the twelfth-century Paisley Abbey to the more modern, but equally striking, housing developments in the town's west end. Like many of the great industrial towns of Scotland, Paisley lost many of its architectural treasures in the name of 1960s progress and modernity. Yet much remains to cherish and celebrate.

As the local MP, I am privileged to represent the people of Paisley and its neighbouring communities. And as a native of Renfrewshire, I am proud to support the work of Ellen Farmer and the Old Paisley Society.

In an age of instant news and the world wide web, it is all too easy to lose sight of our past, of the local people and events that shaped our lives. In *Paisley People & Places* we have the perfect antidote to the stresses of modern times.

I invite you to take time to enjoy this wonderful book and see anew a town bursting with creativity, proud of its heritage but striving forward. That has been the mark of our town – of Paisley and its people – through the ages.

Douglas Alexander MP
Paisley, July 2003

1

Buildings

The Young Men's Christian Association building, built in 1905, at the corner of the High Street and New Street. This is one of the town's finest buildings, even today. The YMCA is still a very active force in the town and encourages young and elderly alike to take part in the community. The range of activities is extensive and includes art classes, men's bowls, boxing and chess, to name a few. The YMCA is also sending eleven young people and four leaders to the YMCA Youth Festival in Prague in 2004. *(Sadie Turnbull)*

Left: This house was photographed on 5 December 1957, when its occupant, a lady of 83, was taken to hospital. We would hope in this day and age that no one would be expected to live in such dreadful conditions as these. *(OPS)*

Below: Galloway Street, 1961. This building was another of those owned by the PCMS and has since been demolished – people returning to Paisley after a long absence would have trouble finding where it had even been. However, memories of being brought up in this street live on: a local man, John Boyle, has written a book about his memories of old Galloway Street and it has been enjoyed by many Paisley Buddies.* *(OPS)*

* The term Paisley Buddy applies to all town folk of Paisley. It is believed to be a corruption of the old Scottish term for bodies. It has been used for many centuries and its origins are now in the dim and distant past. Residents of other towns and cities have their local names, but if you hail from Paisley you are a Buddy.

Brownhall Lodging House in the Sneddon area, 1950. This lodging house was used mainly by men, most of whom were homeless. This was the attic and there were fifteen beds in this one room. There was often a small shop within the lodging house where its occupants could buy the things they needed, usually small amounts of provisions such as tea, sugar and tinned foods. *(OPS)*

This is the washhouse at Brownhall Lodging House – not a very pretty place! However, it did give the men a chance to keep themselves and their clothing clean. The rules and regulations for lodging houses were very severe and the men were strictly regulated about the times they could come in and out. No alcohol was allowed, although many of them probably had a drinking problem . . . and there was strictly no fighting! *(OPS)*

156–148 George Street, 1957. This row of PCMS houses was one of many demolished in the 1950s and 1960s in the centre of the town. George Street was about one mile long and consisted not only of a mixture of houses of this type but also of much nicer Victorian tenement houses. However nostalgic it may be to look back on photographs of these old buildings, not many of us would like to live in such conditions now. *(OPS)*

The PCMS buildings in Causeyside Street, *c.* 1900. At the beginning of its life the PCMS was a small undertaking, but by manufacturing and selling its own goods it grew into a major force in the town, with many shops and factories employing a large number of local people. *(Maurice Irvine)*

The PCMS blouse and underwear factory in Neilston Road. By 1890 it had forty-eight winding, warping, beaming and other machines, and was later further enlarged to take 150 looms as well. The original factory was set up in 1888 in Causeyside Street, but because of the substantial increase in trade, it had to be relocated to Neilston Road. *(Maurice Irvine)*

The PCMS millinery department in about 1910, a time when most women and men, no matter how low their earnings, would not have been seen without a hat, although it was probably the case of the bigger your income the bigger the hat. Nowadays, hats are usually worn only at weddings, garden parties at Holyroodhouse or Ladies Day at Royal Ascot! *(Maurice Irvine)*

One of the town's steepest hills, West Brae, which leads to Oakshaw Street, 1960s. This row of cottages must be among the oldest houses in the town and very picturesque they are too. They are currently empty but it is hoped that they can be adapted for modern-day living, since their demolition would be a dreadful loss to the town. *(OPS)*

West Brae showing the former John Neilston Institution, a school built in 1852 with funds donated by the late John Neilston to improve the education of children. Because of its shape, it is known by the locals as the porridge bowl. As the school became larger, a new one was built and this beautiful building was converted into luxury flats. *(OPS)*

Old houses in Canal Street, 1950. This street was named after the former Paisley Canal, which ran alongside it before the advent of the railways, a quicker and more efficient transport system. These houses had very little sanitation. Indeed, not only were the toilets outside, but, in some cases, so was the water. *(OPS)*

This photograph shows the houses built to replace the ones in the picture above. When the old houses were demolished in the late 1950s and early 1960s, the replacements were classed as luxury. They had bathrooms and central heating and were right in the town centre. Houses in Canal Street are still very much in demand today. *(OPS)*

Snodgrass Mill was a working flour mill and used water power from the River Cart. When the mill closed it was sold to a developer who restored the interior, keeping the waterwheel as a feature in the new hotel's restaurant. Situated in the centre of the town and overlooking the Hammills and the River Cart, this distinctive building, the Watermill Hotel, was saved from the mania for demolition that abounded in the 1950s and 1960s. *(OPS)*

Brown & Polson's was founded in Paisley in the nineteenth century and manufactured cornflour and custard. This is a picture of the Brown & Polson Institute, built by the firm for the recreation of its workforce. The building was used for the workers to meet and socialise. Outside the buildings, the grounds had bowling greens and tennis courts. To the left of the building can be seen some of the houses that the firm built for the workers. The firm was taken over and the work moved to other countries. The factory has now been demolished and is to be replaced by houses. *(OPS)*

A view of the old Paisley Prison, now demolished and replaced by a shopping mall, overlooking the River Cart. At the left of the picture is the Templars Hall, once a beautiful building that at times was used for concerts and musical evenings. The building was constructed in 1826 and could seat around 1,000 people. In later years part of it was used as a cinema and it was in this building that seventy-one children died at a matinée on New Year's Eve 1929. *(OPS)*

Sma' Shot Cottages in George Place were originally built for workers from St Mirren's Mill, which was demolished many years ago. The building was once used as a scouring and bleaching works, but was eventually purchased from Paisley Technical College in 1983 by the Old Paisley Society. The building had lain empty for around eleven years, as can be seen from this view, but has now been restored as an artisans' house, exhibition room and tearoom. *(OPS)*

Sma' Shot Cottages after restoration. The restoration took seven years and was largely done by members and friends of the Old Paisley Society. Behind the cottage garden is an eighteenth-century weaver's cottage, which the Society purchased two years later with money loaned by its members. This interest-free loan was repaid in only four years. Each year the Sma' Shot Cottages Heritage Centre plays host to thousands of visitors who can see how a weaver's family lived in Paisley in the eighteenth and nineteenth centuries. *(OPS)*

The remnants of the old Paisley Canal flow through the site of the Ferguslie Mills, now a housing estate. When the mills were still working, this part of the canal had a thriving population of goldfish that must have been the best-fed fish in Paisley. The mill girls kept bread to feed them on their way back from the canteen, with the result that the fish became so tame they could practically be fed by hand. (J. McSween)

A similar view showing the mill gatehouse now restored and being used as a family home. This is one of the few remaining buildings left on a site that once had nine mills, a fire station, a small first-aid post and many other ancillary buildings. For more than 150 years many men and women passed through this gatehouse on their way to work. (J. McSween)

Thomas Coats Memorial Church is one of the finest Baptist churches in Europe. It was built by the Coats family in memory of Thomas. No expense was spared in its construction and only the finest workmanship and materials were used. The church was completed in 1905 and many a young woman has walked gracefully down the wonderful stairs in her wedding dress. Thanks to a hard-working and active congregation, this wonderful building is still in good repair today. *(OPS)*

Paisley Abbey is the pride of the town, and rightly so. The building was started in 1163 and endowed by Walter, the High Steward of Scotland and father of the Stuart kings and queens. The abbey has played a major part in the history of Scotland. In recent years its medieval drains have been found and important artefacts have come to light, including the oldest piece of written music in Scotland. *(OPS)*

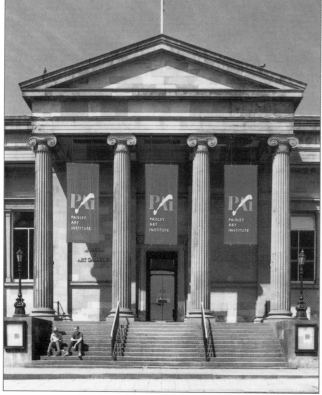

Stables at the entrance to Glen-Coats House in Ferguslie Park, now restored as private homes. When the Coats family left Paisley, the town council used these buildings as storage for its garden equipment. The stables and park were donated to the town for the recreation and enjoyment of the people of Paisley. The park is still used and enjoyed by many people today. (James McSween)

Paisley Museum and Art Galleries house the finest collection of Paisley shawls in the world. The museum, completed in 1871, was built partly to house the collection of items gathered over many years by the Paisley Philosophical Society and was funded largely by the Coats family. It also has wonderful collections of pottery, paintings and local history items, as well as a complete edition of *Audubon's Birds of America*. However, the large stuffed elephant that was once a great favourite of the children of the town has now turned to dust. (Paisley Museum)

2

Shops & Industry

Staff of the British and Argentine Meat Company, at Wellmeadow Street. The premises later housed Alex Munro Limited, but the building is now demolished. The person on the right is Robert Kyle, manager in about 1925. Supermarkets and out-of-town shopping centres have seen the end of small local butcher's shops.
(Paisley Museum)

This was Paisley's largest and finest department store, designed by local architect J. Steel Maitland in the art-deco style. Although the interior was modernised over the years, becoming part of the House of Fraser group in the 1960s, the frontage still retained its distinctive art-deco design. In the tearoom, if you had a window seat, you would have a beautiful view of the abbey and town hall – one of the finest views in the town. The store closed in 2004, a great loss to the town.
(Paisley Museum)

Above: Here is another example of the work of the architect J. Steel Maitland. This dress shop was popular among Paisley women and girls. During the 1950s and 1960s, the High Street was very busy and had many shops catering for all tastes and pockets. Paisley people could complete their shopping here, be it for food, shoes, wallpaper, ironmongery or clothing. Times have now changed: people are now more mobile and have different shopping habits. *(Paisley Museum)*

Opposite above: Mary Ann McCance's grocery shop at 22 Glen Street, 1940s. Thomas McCance, Mary Ann's husband, could do only light work, his lungs having been damaged by dust during his work as a stonemason. Sadly, Mr McCance died shortly after buying the store, and, as there was no widow's pension in those days, Mrs McCance had to continue working to support herself and her son. *(Ann Philpot)*

Opposite below: Members of the family outside the shop in Glen Street. Mrs McCance was seen to be a soft touch when it came to giving credit. She would give bread and other groceries to people who said, 'My weans are starving. I will pay you later.' However, when she tried to get the debts owed to her, the same people would cross the street to avoid her. How often must this have happened to small shopkeepers! *(Ann Philpot)*

Galbraith's Stores in Paisley, *c.* 1930. Galbraith's was a local grocery firm with branches all over the town, and it also had factories where employees made the company's own brand of soups, pickles and jams. Galbraith's was taken over by Safeway in the late 1960s, and its small shops and factories were closed. *(Paisley Museum)*

A presentation to a member of staff at Galbraith's Store in Cotton Street, Paisley, *c.* 1953. Perhaps she was leaving to go to another store. Perhaps she was being promoted. Perhaps she was even emigrating. Whatever the occasion, her fellow workers would have collected money to give her a going-away gift. *(Agnes McLean)*

Kendalls and Dunn & Company in the High Street, 1958 – a nostalgic view of shops that will bring back memories to many Paisley Buddies. Kendalls was frequented by many mill girls, whose good wages allowed them to shop in a store that sold clothes that were a bit more stylish and expensive than average. Many young women bought their going-away outfits here for their honeymoon. Dunn's is a reminder of the days when men wore hats, caps and Harris tweed jackets. *(Paisley Museum)*

McGlashan's shop in Moss Street, 1920s. The staff outside are posing happily for the camera. This was a well-known shop in the town, and by the look of the stock in the window, the staff made sure you didn't walk out empty handed. In Moss Street you could buy almost anything, from garden and household fittings, to toys and ice-cream. *(OPS)*

The staff at Gilmour Street station in the mid-nineteenth century. It took a large staff in those days to run a railway station: plumbers, ticket staff, engineers, cleaners and many others were employed. The station was a busy one, with regular trains to Glasgow, Greenock, Ayr and most seaside towns in the area. The first fortnight in August was 'The Paisley Fair' holiday, when the station would be crowded with families heading for their summer break. The stationmaster at this time was John Workman. *(Paisley Museum)*

The railway bridge at Gilmour Street in the 1850s. This station has, of course, expanded over the years, but many of the out-of-town stations have been closed, cutting the service to several towns and villages in Renfrewshire. *(Paisley Museum)*

Clark Hunter's cooperage in Greenhill Road, 1950s. Founded in 1875, this business is now closed, but at one time it was the largest cooperage in Paisley, owned and run by the Hunter family. As the picture shows, the railway ran alongside the cooperage and at the top of the image is a row of Edwardian terraced houses, built by the Hunter family around 1906 and rented out. Nowadays the houses are owner-occupied. The prefabs in the foreground have now disappeared. *(Margaret Hunter)*

This is an older picture of the cooperage, taken in the 1920s when the majority of the barrels were wooden. Note the use of advertising boards along the fence. Like many local businessmen, the Hunters played their part in local life and took a great pride in this activity. Mr Clark Hunter, author and historian, was particularly eminent, and when he died he left a legacy of fine paintings and artefacts to the town. *(Margaret Hunter)*

A 1960s advertisement for the cooperage, showing the change from wooden barrels to aluminium and other materials. It indicates that, like many other firms, Clark Hunter adapted to modern materials and methods. Wooden barrels are now used mainly for whisky and sherry. However, the cooperage is gone and the site is now a lorry park. *(Sally McMillan)*

A Clark Hunter's horse and cart outside the cooperage. The horses were stabled in Park Buildings, Underwood Lane, and in 1890 there was a horse-trotting track at the north end of Paisley. If you wanted to see a gentleman called Byron Smith for a stock horse for breeding, this was the place to come. According to his advertisement, he was at the Paisley Stables every day except Wednesday! *(Margaret Hunter)*

Stonefield Laundry was situated in Lochfield Road. This beautiful horse and its decorated cart were used for advertising in about 1900, but the washing was delivered all over the town by this mode of transport. In the days before washing-machines and tumble-driers, laundries were used by a great many people. If you could afford it, you would send everything to the laundry – shirts, sheets, underwear, socks, table covers, pillowcases. *(Margaret Hunter)*

The Viyella Factory in Seedhill Road, 1960s. This was one of the last textile works in Paisley. At one time textile mills and factories were spread throughout the town. As time went on, however, it was cheaper for firms to transfer either to England or overseas, so that slowly the mills and factories all disappeared from Paisley. We, like others all over Britain, have had to adapt to job losses. *(OPS)*

The cranes of Fleming & Ferguson's shipyard. Although shipbuilding was mainly concentrated in Glasgow, at one time Paisley had several shipbuilders, including Bow & McLaughlin and Bar & McNab. One of Bow & McLaughlin's ships can still be seen in Victoria, British Columbia, Canada, and is now a floating restaurant in a dock. Fleming & Ferguson closed in 1968. *(OPS)*

Dobies cigarette factory in Greenhill Road, now Carlton Die Castings. This building is built in the art-deco style, although here it looks a bit neglected. Perhaps one day it will be restored. The brandname for Dobies cigarettes was 'Four Square', indicating that when you bought the product, you were getting a square deal – not a politically correct ideal today! When Dobies closed down, the factory was reused by BMK carpets and is still in use today by an engineering firm. *(Brian Jolly)*

The cigarette room at Dobies, 1948. This was a time when jobs were easier to come by than they are now. The fact that the factory was owned by a local family was a mixed blessing: the family knew most of its employees, and if you were a good timekeeper and a hard worker, it would employ other members of your family. If you weren't liked, it could work against you. *(Paisley Museum)*

The leaf room at Dobies, 1949. Here the girls separated and graded the leaves. Dobies had a very good relationship with their staff, and the girls themselves, as was usual in factories at that time, were friends as well as workmates. *(Paisley Museum)*

A visit to the factory by Scottish comedian and actor Duncan McCrae. He was a well-known and much-loved entertainer, and his visit was a great event and a welcome break for the workers. In the 1950s and 1960s many factories invited stage and screen actors to visit in order to boost workers' morale and give the actors free publicity. *(Paisley Museum)*

3

Special Days

Members of the Old Paisley Society at the abbey in 1988. They are dressed in crinolines and, of course, Paisley shawls. In 1988 Paisley celebrated its 500th year as a Burgh of Barony and many events were organised to mark the anniversary. Queen Elizabeth planted a Paisley Anniversary rose and, accompanied by the Duke of Edinburgh, attended a service at the abbey. *(I. Gilbert)*

The crowds lined the streets for the Queen's first visit to Paisley since her coronation in 1953. People waited hours to get a good view. It was a very hot day and the first-aiders were kept busy helping those who fainted because of the temperature or who had been standing too long. However, all were pleased to get a glimpse of their young queen and her husband. *(OPS)*

The former Junior Section of the Old Paisley Society, 1980s. The youngsters are dressed in Victorian period costume ready to receive visitors to the annual Sma' Shot Cottages fundraising Christmas party. Guests are served a traditional Scottish supper and then entertained with carol singing and a visit from Santa Claus. This event has been a sell-out for the past eighteen years, and there is always a waiting list. *(OPS)*

Another fundraising event at Sma' Shot cottages. Concerts are held (weather permitting) in the walled garden of the cottages. Initiated by the folk singer, (the late) Danny Kyle, they are now organised by musician and broadcaster Davy Scott, who, like Danny, brings along friends to help with the entertainment. The musicians all give their services free of charge, as do the birds in the cottage garden, who have been known to join in. *(OPS)*

There was always a great sense of community in housing estates in the 1950s and early 1960s. These Shortroods tenants are making their way to Gilmour Street station for their annual outing to the seaside. It was a real family day out and everyone looked forward to it. *(Ann Wilson)*

Shortroods people holding the banner that would precede them to the station. Tenants' associations, some still in existence today, organised many events for the people in their area. Members also looked after each other and would help solve many problems in their areas, liaising with town councillors to help sort out any difficulties. *(Ann Wilson)*

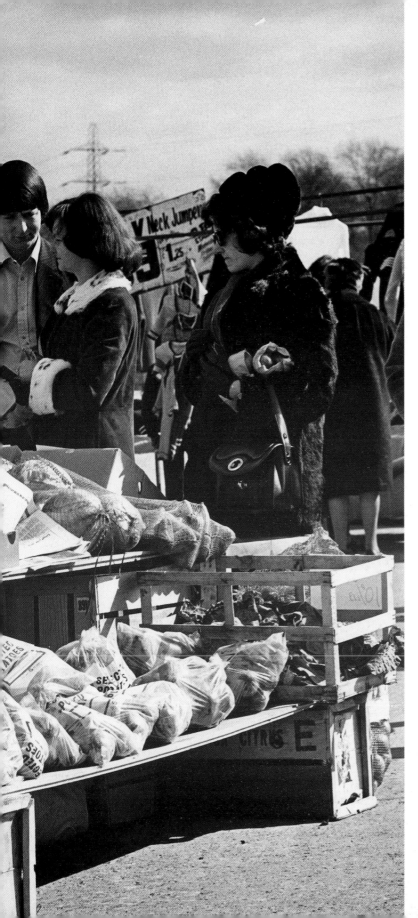

A Sunday market at Glenfield Road, 1975. The market was held at Wilson's, the cattle auctioneers, and it was a very popular weekly event, but was discontinued because of protests by house owners in the area. The traffic was heavy, and, although the market took place only once a week, it did cause disruption. Now, however, Paisley has a very popular farmers' market, held in the town centre twice a month. *(OPS)*

A fairground, possibly in an area known as the Clayholes, *c.* 1890. As in most towns, fairs have a long history. For many years now, during Paisley Fair holidays, a funfair has been held at St James Park, the site of the old Paisley racecourse. Although not as large as it once was, the fair is still popular with local people. *(Paisley Museum)*

The old cattle market in St James Street, *c.* 1890. It later moved to Storie Street and was held there until the early 1960s. It then moved to Glenfield Road but sadly has now moved out of the town completely. Many people in the town remember the cattle and sheep being driven down the High Street in the 1940s, but the traffic was a bit lighter then! *(Paisley Museum)*

Anchor Mills Lawn Bowling League. Were the ladies heading off for an outing or an away match? They had their own beautiful bowling green at Anchor Mills, and the workers at Ferguslie Mill had one too. Now that Coats Mills are demolished and Clarks Mill has moved out of the area, their bowling greens are privately owned. *(OPS)*

The 50th Annual Conference of the Scottish YMCA, held between 7 and 9 October 1927. This photograph was taken on the steps of the Thomas Coats Memorial Church. The town has one of the most beautiful YMCA buildings in the country, and many other members were no doubt impressed by the Paisley branch's headquarters. *(YMCA)*

The residents of St James Avenue holding a garden party to celebrate the end of the First World War. St James Avenue was built by the owner of the Clark Hunter cooperage and consists of a row of Edwardian terraced houses constructed between 1906 and 1908. The avenue was built on land that used to be part of Paisley racecourse. The whole of the

racecourse area was ultimately bought by the Burgh Council, and much of it became St James Park. However, as land was required to construct the motorway and St James interchange, the bowling greens and tennis courts disappeared. St James Avenue is now completely separated from the park. *(Edward Farmer)*

The last meeting of Paisley Burgh Council, 1975. With the reorganisation of local councils and the creation of Strathclyde Regional Council, Paisley became a part of the new Renfrew District Council along with other towns and villages in the area. However, nothing lasts for ever, and Strathclyde Region no longer exists either. The town is now part of Renfrewshire Council. *(OPS)*

The seventieth anniversary of the Glen Cinema disaster, 1999. The tragedy happened in 1929, when seventy-one children died on New Year's Eve. As a canister of film started to smoulder, panic set in and the children, who tried to get out of locked doors, were crushed. Laying the wreath is Provost John McDowell and also present are descendants of families who were affected by the accident all those years ago. It is touching to see children being brought by their parents to remember relatives they have never known but whose memories continue to be kept alive. *(OPS)*

4

Paisley Fire Brigade

The first known Paisley fire brigade was formed in 1677. Paisley was just a village then and most of the houses had thatched roofs. In 1833 the captain of Paisley fire brigade was Alexander Wallace and his deputy was William Wallace. The fire engines were housed at the meat market in Weigh House Close, but were later housed in Gilmour Street opposite the prison. Keys were kept at the prison and at the captain's house in the High Street. This picture was probably taken in the 1950s. *(Alex Imrie)*

The town's first purpose-built fire station opened on 13 April 1899. The fire engines had previously been housed at Abbey Close in 1869 and in 1877 were moved to a property in Moss Street that had once been the stables for the Saracen's Head inn. The firemen's station was in another property in Moss Street; it was entered through a pend at no. 5 and is now a tobacconist's shop. *(Alex Imrie)*

This Humber saloon car is towing a Coventry Climax tractor pump, which was stationed at Wallace's Garage in East Lane and was used by the auxiliary fire service, formed in 1939. The fire master at that time was Robert Bowman OBE: when he took up his position in 1937 he inherited a full-time staff of around thirty-three. (*Alex Imrie*)

The same Humber car. The hose and ladder holder was made in the brigade workshops. At the start of the Second World War, men throughout the whole of Britain were recruited to 'man' the brigade in emergencies, many of them after finishing a shift at their factory or office. During the war the brigade headquarters were in the Johnston Street fire station and the control centre was at Moredun House at the south end of Paisley.
(*Alex Imrie*)

This Lagonda saloon car, with two wooden ladders and towing a Harland tractor pump, was stationed at Bell's Laundry during the Second World War. The car was donated to the fire service by an Elderslie bookmaker, no doubt a welcome gift to a country at war, short of money and in need of all the help it could get. (*Alex Imrie*)

It was not all depression at this anxious time. This is Plug, the mascot of the firemen at Bell's Laundry. He was named after the fire plugs (hydrants) in the streets. Here he is quite happily chewing on a fireman's boot. Let's hope he had permission to enjoy it. (*Alex Imrie*)

Fire Master Alex Girdwood and his crew at the fire station in Johnston Street, 1926. Mr Girdwood was well known in Paisley and a film survives that shows he was something of a daredevil when it came to scaling the station's ladders. Presumably it was made to demonstrate his firefighting skills. Mr Girdwood's funeral was one of the largest the town had seen in many years, and it was testament to the respect the town had for him and his crew. *(Tom Brown)*

A promotional picture of the Western Area fire brigade taken in 1963. This was now a much better equipped brigade (see pages 56–7), although some of the engines were still of a great age. From left to right those pictured are a 1941 Leyland Merryweather, a 1955 Dennis F8 (Paisley retained machine), a 1955 Dennis F7 (Paisley full-time machine) and a Dennis F12 pump escape. The watch-room girls are in the main door with the watch-room just behind them. *(Alex Imrie)*

Station Officer Adam Bisset and the watch-room girls at the Western Area fire brigade in Johnston Street. Note the large control panel and clock. The flaps on the board would drop if an alarm was sounded in any of the major risk areas in town. The turn-out alarm would then be set off from the watch-room. *(Alex Imrie)*

An exercise in George Street, 1950s. This photograph was taken when the George Street area of the town was being redeveloped. The reconstruction work gave Paisley's retained fire brigade an opportunity to practise the skills they needed in emergencies. The man looking towards the camera is Leading Fireman Alex Imrie, who was in charge of Paisley's retained crew. (*Alex Imrie*)

Another view of the George Street exercise showing a close-up of a Bedford pump. The women on the right are part of the St Andrew's Ambulance Service. Children and adults alike enjoyed the spectacle of the practice exercise. (*Alex Imrie*)

A children's Christmas party held in Paisley fire station, 1948. At this time it was common practice for organisations to hold parties like this for the children of their staff, which proved exciting not only for the children but also for their parents! There were no theme parks or television in those days, the world being a

much less sophisticated place than it is now. It was a time for girls to wear party dresses and boys to be cleaned up and put into their best clothes. *(Alex Imrie)*

A retained crew at Paisley fire station with trophies won at ladder and pump competitions. These men worked hard to achieve the standards required to win their trophies. The retained firemen were used as a back-up to the full-time fire brigade. Each man had a bell in his home, which was rung by the fire station when he was required. The men were only paid when they turned out for a fire or an exercise. There are still retained firefighters in parts of Renfrewshire. *(Alex Imrie)*

Many different vehicles were used during the Second World War. This is an Austin taxi that towed a tractor pump and its wooden ladders. This vehicle always ran with its windows down because there was a leak in the exhaust and fumes came up into the cab. The man standing next to the taxi is Tom McFarlane. *(Alex Imrie)*

5

Music & Drama

Yin for the Abbot, written for the Paisley Players by author and playwright Evelyn Hood. Music and drama have for long been dear to townspeople: the Paisley Players were formed in 1905 and the Paisley Musical and Operatic Society was founded in 1908. *(Paisley Players)*

Like many clubs of its kind, the Paisley Players group was formed for 'the mental improvement of its members, the cultivation of literary taste and the study of dramatic art' – high ideals indeed. The Players have performed in all the main venues in Paisley, including the Town Hall and the Arts Centre. In 2005 they will celebrate their centenary. *(Paisley Players)*

The reception given by the Provost and Council to celebrate the Paisley Players' ninetieth anniversary, 1995. It takes a great deal of hard work, determination and dedication for a club like this to keep going in the twenty-first century. Tastes have changed since the advent of television, and people are sometimes reluctant to leave their homes in the evening. Fortunately there are still many people prepared to support the Players and keen to keep the tradition going. *(Paisley Players)*

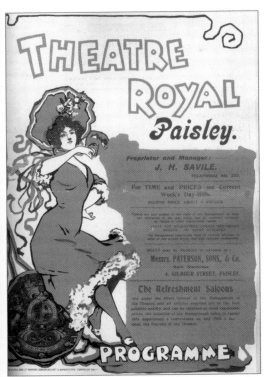

Left: The cover of a programme for the Theatre Royal, now long gone. Printers used to go to a great deal of trouble to make programmes attractive, and the Paisley Players no doubt hoped they could attract the sponsors required to help pay for the work. The management of the theatre went to great lengths to tell the customers that the refreshments available were reasonable, of good value and priced to please rather than provide profit! *(Paisley Players)*

Below left: A notice advertising a dramatic recital by the Players in aid of the War Heroes' Fund in 1919. Most amateur companies have always raised money for charities of all kinds. At this period the War Heroes' Fund was a popular cause. It helped the soldiers who had returned from the First World War. *(Paisley Players)*

Below: A programme for a play performed in 1925 at the Central Halls. The reverse of the programme lists former productions, including J.M. Barrie's *The Little Minister,* and gives the names of people involved in the production. *(Paisley Players)*

WAR HEROES' FUND.

A

DRAMATIC RECITAL

BY THE

PAISLEY PLAYERS' CLUB.

WILL BE GIVEN IN THE

Town Hall, Johnstone,

ON

FRIDAY, 31ST JANUARY, 1919.

DOORS OPEN AT 7-15.   COMMENCE AT 7-45 P.M.

TICKETS 2/- AND 1/-

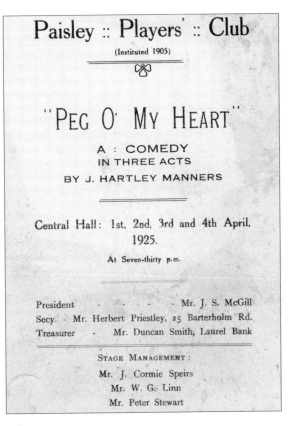

Paisley :: Players' :: Club
(Instituted 1905)

"PEG O' MY HEART"

A : COMEDY
IN THREE ACTS
BY J. HARTLEY MANNERS

Central Hall: 1st, 2nd, 3rd and 4th April, 1925.

At Seven-thirty p.m.

President   -   -   -   - Mr. J. S. McGill
Secy. - Mr. Herbert Priestley, 25 Barterholm Rd.
Treasurer   -   Mr. Duncan Smith, Laurel Bank

STAGE MANAGEMENT :
Mr. J. Cormie Speirs
Mr. W. G. Linn
Mr. Peter Stewart

A very serious-looking play, 1920s. Note how well dressed the cast are and how well furnished the set, with wood panelling and posh furniture. These items were donated by local shops in return for a credit in the programme. *(Paisley Players)*

OFFICE-BEARERS.

Hon. President
Sir J. Martin Harvey

Hon. Vice-Presidents
Rev. Walter A. Mursell
E. S. Coats, Esq.
George H. Coats, Esq.
J. M. Lang, Esq., LL.B.
Lord Glentanar

President
Mr J. Lavis Angus

Vice-Presidents
Mr Wm. M'Gregor   Mr R. Thorburn

Secretary
Mr Herbert Priestley, 8 Glen View

Treasurer
Mr James K. M'Rory, Tower Buildings

Property Masters
Mr James Comrie Speirs & Mr W. Linn

Assistant Property Masters
Mr Peter Stewart

Committee

Mr D. W. Crawford	Mr J. D. Wardrop
,, Chas. Donochy	,, Jas Black
,, Duncan Smith	,, John Marshall
,, M. MacLachlan	,, J. S. M'Gill

MONTHLY MEETINGS
in George Hotel, at 8 p.m.

1922
Wednesday,   Oct. 11th
    do.   Nov. 8th.
    do.   Dec. 13th.
1923
Wednesday,   Jan. 10th.
    do.   Feb. 14th.
    do.   Mar. 14th.

Pianist .. Mr A. C. PHIPPS.

Syllabus for 1922–3. Note the distinguished names involved in the club, including members of the Coats family. The Hon. President, Sir John Martin Harvey, was a famous actor in his day. The Players met in the George Hotel, which is now long gone. Whether the pianist was there to entertain the members or for rehearsal is not known – perhaps both.
(Paisley Players)

This picture was taken in 1920, when membership of Paisley Players was much larger than it is now.
(Paisley Players)

The reverse of a programme showing the sponsors of the Paisley Players. Before the days of multinational shops and out-of-town shopping centres, the town was filled with locally run stores whose owners would probably take part in theatrical activities themselves and so had an interest in supporting them. However, society has moved on and people have to adapt to the changes. We are proud to say that Paisley Players have managed to do just that. *(Paisley Players)*

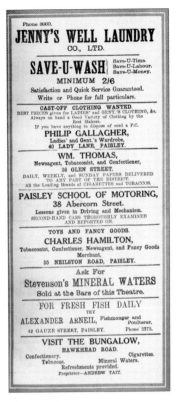

On stage at Gallowhill Community Centre, 1990s. The Players still manage to dress their sets and their actors well, but it is becoming harder for amateur dramatic groups to finance productions. They occasionally receive grants from the Lottery Fund and Renfrewshire Council, but have to raise the rest themselves. *(Paisley Players)*

The Paisley Musical and Operatic Society was formed at a meeting held in the George Temperance Hotel in July 1908. This photograph was taken at a performance of *Mame* in 2002 in the King's Theatre in Glasgow. *(PMOS)*

The programme for the PMOS's performance of *The Gondoliers* held at Paisley Theatre in 1926. From 1908 until 1923 the society produced various comic operas. Between 1923 and 1964, however, it was a purely Gilbert and Sullivan club. The programme is colourful and typical of the period. Like the Paisley Players' programme on page 69, it is filled with adverts for local shops and businesses. It also lists all the performers and production staff. (PMOS)

The cast and production team for a show at Paisley Theatre in 1926. In 1959 the society staged its last performance in the theatre, which was then closed down and later demolished. The group then performed in various venues in Glasgow – as one member said, they became 'wandering minstrels'! However, in 1968, the year of the society's diamond jubilee, it found a permanent home in the King's Theatre, Glasgow. *(OPS)*

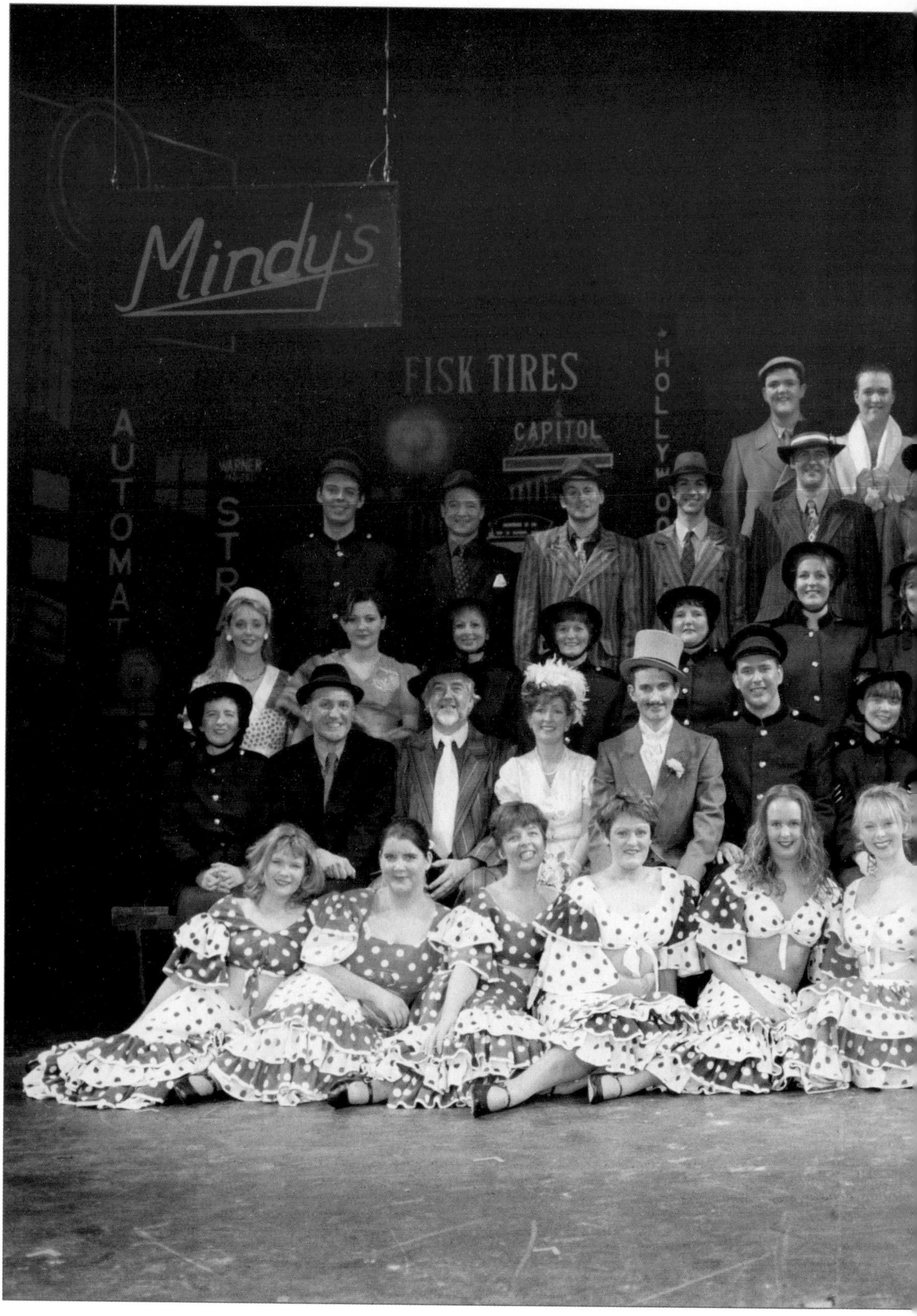
Mindy's
FISK TIRES
CAPITOL
AUTOMAT

This picture was taken at the performance of *Guys and Dolls* in 1999. Performing at the King's in Glasgow is wonderful, but is a luxury the society can ill afford. Unfortunately Paisley no longer has a theatre large enough to stage PMOS shows. The Town Hall is used for concerts and musical events, but there are not enough dressing rooms for a large cast. *(PMOS)*

A great deal of effort is required to fill the number of seats necessary to fund the use of the King's, and the society works hard all year, not just in rehearsals but selling tickets and performing at smaller venues in order to encourage people to attend large productions. This picture shows the cast of *My Fair Lady* in 2000. *(PMOS)*

The *Mikado*, performed when the society was largely a Gilbert and Sullivan club. The PMOS is still a thriving group and its members enjoy each and every performance, giving great pleasure to the thousands of people who travel to see them every year. In a few years' time both the Paisley Players and the Paisley Musical and Operatic Society will be celebrating their centenary – Paisley Players in 2005 and Paisley Musical and Operatic Society in 2008. *(PMOS)*

The Paisley Youth Theatre was formed in 1988 and helps keep alive the town's enthusiasm for music and drama. PACE Theatre Company is the largest of its kind in Scotland. Its various sections – PACE Youth Theatre, PACE Casting and PACE Media Productions – all complement and work with each other for the benefit of children aged between 5 and 18. This picture shows a workshop at PACE's base in the Wynd Centre. *(PACE)*

A scene from *The Lords of Creation*, performed in October 2001. PACE was formed to encourage and teach children the arts of acting, producing and writing, and its members have performed all over Scotland. *(PACE)*

The Legend of Dragonara, performed in May 2003. PACE has provided young actors for many film and TV companies. Its members have appeared in *Monarch of the Glen*, *Strictly Sinatra* and *The Slab Boys*. No doubt it will continue to bring forward many other talented young people in the future. *(PACE)*

Another scene from *The Legend of Dragonara*. PACE is also commissioned each year by Renfrewshire Council to take part in the town's unique traditional Sma' Shot Day; its students write and produce the story of the Paisley weavers. PACE has already produced one young star – the winner of BBC's *Fame Academy*, David Sneddon. *(PACE)*

6

Italian Buddies

Most towns in Scotland have an Italian connection and Paisley is certainly fortunate
in its Italian community. Many Italian families have been in the town for almost a
100 years and have contributed, and are still contributing, a great deal to the
town's economy. This picture of a Nardini's ice-cream cart outside La Dolce Vita café
and restaurant is a nostalgic reminder of the way many Italian families started out
in Paisley. The owner of La Dolce Vita preserves the old tradition by displaying this
bicycle-powered cart outside his premises in Moss Street. Paisley can claim the
Nardini family among its past inhabitants – they started their famous ice-cream
business here some years ago. *(Sadie Turnbull)*

Giuseppe Pieraccini arrived in Paisley from Barga in 1904 with the clothes on his back, some bread for the journey and no English whatsoever. He started work with a fellow Italian in what became Cardosi's café in Causeyside Street. In 1909 he took a lease on a shop in Johnston Street and opened St George's Fish Restaurant. The Pieraccinis were on their way! This is the interior of the restaurant, all chrome and tiles in typical 1930s style. (*Carla Mialina*)

In the early years the Pieraccinis lived across the road from their St George's Fish Restaurant, but, as the family grew, so did the business, and they opened another shop in Mill Street. This was a wise move, because they were now in a good position to serve the thousands of mill workers. *(Piero Pieraccini)*

The interior of the family restaurant in Mill Street, with all its gleaming art-deco fittings, which not only looked good but were also easy to keep clean. Piero Pieraccini's father Joe is in the centre with Piero's mother on the right and cousin Gina on the left. Note all the sweets on the shelves: this photograph was obviously taken before the start of the Second World War and the introduction of rationing. *(Piero Pieraccini)*

The interior of the shop with Joe Pieraccini and cousin Attilio, who is holding the pet monkey! Children took great delight in meeting this little creature. Nowadays, of course, for health and safety reasons it would not be allowed into the shop. Safety is now a top priority, but does that make life a little more boring for us all? *(Piero Pieraccini)*

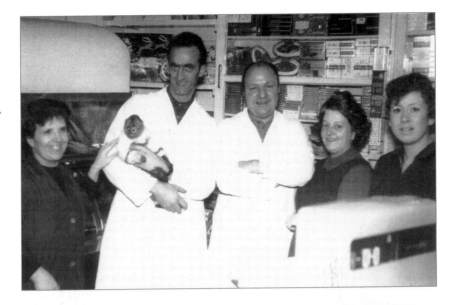

Joe Pieraccini and his wife Fausta celebrating their golden wedding surrounded by their children. Standing from the left are Gino, Meri, Ada, Iole and Mario. Life in Scotland was tough for them at first, coming to a new country and starting a new life. During the Second World War, Joe and Fausta saw their two sons interned in the Isle of Man. The policeman who came to arrest Mario had attended school with him and it was a great embarrassment to them both. Times have changed and here the couple sit surrounded by their children, a happy and successful family. Their wedding anniversary was celebrated in Barga. *(Piero Pieraccini)*

Piero outside his bar, Hamish's Hoose. Although most of the Pierracini family have worked in the restaurant trade, the only ones serving the public today are Piero, Mario, Constanza's son, and Nadia, Gino's youngest daughter. Nadia runs the Craigielea Bar in Wellmeadow Street. Piero is very much involved in the town. He is chair of the Paisley Traders and of the Paisley Development Association. He may have Italian roots, but his heart is now firmly in Paisley. *(Piero Pieraccini)*

The Italian families in Paisley moved with the times and their shops reflected this. This is the wonderful (and modern for its time) art-deco café in Gauze Street in the 1930s. In 1934 the Italian families settled in Lawn Street and also had shops in Canal Street, George Street, Glasgow Road and Broomlands. Pasquale and Elvira Napolitano arrived in Scotland in 1915, and, with hard work and the help of their family, they prospered. They owned the East End Café. *(Ricardo Napolitano)*

A Napolitano family ice-cream van, early 1950s. The vans travelled round the streets selling ice-cream and sweets. People listened out for the (usually) musical chimes that annouced a van's arrival. Some would come out of their houses with jugs to be filled with ice-cream, the level to which the jug was filled being determined by the amount paid. This ice-cream then became a family's teatime pudding. Not many people had fridges in those days, so ice-cream had to be bought and used immediately. Of course, the vans also sold the usual ice-cream cones and nugget wafers too – cones for the children and chocolate nuggets for mum and dad. *(Ricardo Napolitano)*

The Italians were, and are, famous for their ice-cream and each family had its own recipes. For many young Paisley Buddies it was a special treat to be taken for an ice-cream after church on Sundays. Teenagers also enjoyed the cafés in those days, when you were allowed to spend hours talking to your friends for the cost of a coffee and a few pence for the jukebox. *(Ricardo Napolitano)*

The Napolitanos' Eastern Café in Glasgow Road. There was barely a street in Paisley that didn't have an Italian café. All their ice-cream was homemade and everyone in Paisley had their favourite: they would argue about who made the best ice-cream, but usually favoured the shop they visited themselves, of course! During the Second World War ice-cream makers had to cope with rationing and shortages. They compromised by using powdered egg and dried milk instead of fresh ingredients and managed to continue to supply the public. *(Carla Mialina)*

Staff outside the Napolitanos' East End Café. Note the nice clean overalls the girls are wearing. Pasquale Napolitano was interned during the war, as were many Italians, including members of the Conti and Porrelli families. Most of them were sent to the Isle of Man. This must have been a very difficult time for those left behind – the men were taken away and the women were left to cope with the children and the business. However, they all managed to survive the experience and are now an important part of life in Paisley. *(Ricardo Napolitano)*

The queue outside the shop shows how good the ice-cream was, but it is also a sign of how times have changed. People still buy the ice-cream but now store it in freezers, rather than eating it straight away. *(Ricardo Napolitano)*

Napolitano's today – no longer just a café but mainly a carry-out and home-delivery business, selling everything from traditional fish and chips to pizzas, curries and many other foods too. The tradition of service is still alive and well among families who have served their community for almost 100 years. *(Ricardo Napolitano)*

THE PORRELLI STORY

Gerardo and Carolina Porrelli left San Biagia in southern Italy in 1920 to come to Scotland. Gerardo began working in a café in Lawn Street, which was owned by Mr Rossi. When Mr Rossi retired after a few years, he offered the business to Gerardo, and this is where Porrelli's ice-cream was born. Both Gerardo and Carolina went around the streets of Paisley selling ice-cream from a wheelbarrow and a horse and cart. This was back-breaking work that entailed starting early in the morning to make the ice-cream, and they also ran the café.

The Porrellis had four children, Leonita (born 1924), Guido (born 1927), Italina (born 1929) and the youngest, Gina (born 1932). As the family got older, they all lent a hand in running the café, serving the customers by standing on wooden crates that enabled them to reach the counter.

In those days the Italians received a lot of abuse. There was frequently trouble in the shop and windows were often smashed. In time things settled down and on account of their efforts and likeable nature they were accepted into the community. However, when the Second World War came, all immigrants, including the Porrellis, were interned. Initially Gerardo was sent to Edinburgh, from where he was scheduled to go to Canada on the *Andorra Star*, but he broke his foot and could not travel. He was then sent to the Isle of Man. Carolina and the family had to move to Glasgow.

When the war ended, Gerardo came back to Paisley and together the family got back behind the business again. Sadly, Carolina became seriously ill in 1945 and died, leaving her husband with a young family. In 1955 the Porrellis opened another café in Ferguslie and then the Skaters Café in Glasgow Road. At that time, this was the 'in' place to be for bikers, teddy boys and ice skaters. In 1959 the Porrellis moved to Underwood Lane, where they converted a small dairy into a factory that produced ice-cream and ice lollies. From there they also started operating ice-cream vans servicing the Paisley area, all the family again being involved. Gerardo remarried. His new bride was a widow called Angelina, whose son Gianni also made a significant contribution to the development of the business.

Porrelli's moved to its present site in Lacy Street in 1969. The business developed into a wholesale outlet, and distributed ice-cream and desserts to a variety of customers. Today the company is managed by Gerardo's grandson, Enzo Durante, and still practises according to the same principles of good quality and hard work. Although it is still a family business, there are no longer as many family members involved. The company presently employs fourteen people and distributes ice-cream and desserts all over Scotland, supplying hotels, restaurants, cafés, wholesalers and, most recently, Asda.

7

Sports & Hobbies

Young Hugh Goudie practising his batting skills in the yard at his father's business at 10 Maxwelton Street, 1950s. The Goudie family have owned an undertakers here for many years. The sports and hobbies that were popular in Paisley at this time ranged from the serious to the amusing, from archery to cricket, curling, yachting, music, football and netball – the list was endless. *(Morag Goudie)*

Paisley Amateur
Swimming Club, 1920.
These young men were
Scottish water polo
champions, and were
proud to pose with the
cups they had won. At
one time Paisley had a
great swimming
tradition and produced
many champions.
Unfortunately, the
town's swimming baths
were demolished in the
early 1970s and
replaced by a modern
fun pool, great for
children but not so good
for the serious swimmer.
Consequently, in the late
1970s Paisley Swimming
Club was disbanded.
(OPS)

Youngsters from Paisley YMCA learning archery, 1970s. They seem to be thoroughly enjoying themselves, having fun while learning a new skill. The YMCA still plays a large part in encouraging young people to learn new sports and pastimes to keep their minds and bodies active. *(Paisley YMCA)*

Fun and games playing netball . . . or is it basketball? Here more young people from the YMCA are enjoying themselves, this time outdoors. This looks like a much healthier occupation than spending hours on computer games, although no doubt many young people do both. *(Paisley YMCA)*

Motor-cross racing on the Gleniffer Braes, an exciting sport but one that is no longer practised in Paisley. In the 1970s it was very popular, but could also be dangerous. Gleniffer Braes is well known in the town and has been used for recreation for many years. In the eighteenth century it was a popular place for walks, just as it is today. *(OPS)*

Another view of motor-cross showing some of the riders ready for action. The views from Gleniffer Braes are stunning and many people visit the park for this reason alone. Renfrewshire Council has a ranger service providing guided walks based on themes, including flora and fauna, archaeology and history. *(OPS)*

The restoration of this boat on the quay at Paisley harbour was a hobby for architect Duncan Adam. It took over three years to restore the boat, but, with the help of friends, the project was completed in 1982. The River Cart sees few yachts now, as it has largely silted up. However, in recent years a local society, the Paisley Canal and Waterways Society, run by volunteers, has played a part in encouraging restoration and cleaning up the old quayside. Members of the society have taken little boats well up into the town on occasion. *(Di Adam)*

Skipper Duncan Adam aboard his boat, the restoration completed at last! Now the boat is ready to take the family and friends who helped make it seaworthy. Of the many hobbies people enjoy, Duncan's must be one of the most ambitious. Like many town harbours, Paisley's has had some refurbishment in the last few years. *(Di Adam)*

A model naval ship display in Barshaw Park, 1981. Barshaw is a popular park and is used for many events throughout the year. Much fun is still to be had on Barshaw's boating pond. *(Alex Imrie)*

Model naval ships at Barshaw pond, 1981. Hundreds of people gathered to see the vessels, which were built to scale and painted in the regulation battleship grey. The owners spent many hours preparing for this display and their reward was the spectators' enjoyment. *(Alex Imrie)*

Sailing a yacht at Barshaw pond in the 1950s or early 1960s. This was a favourite hobby among children at this time. At the weekend it could get pretty crowded, with fathers and sons busy racing their yachts against each other. The pond was only a small part of the park: tennis courts were (and still are) widely used, as was the golf course. Music festivals and concerts also take place here. *(Alex Imrie)*

This little boy plays alone in his home, working on his Meccano set, 1950s. He is concentrating on building what looks like a crane as he sits in front of an old cast-iron range in what was probably a tenement house. He looks cosy and comfortable, using his stool as a work bench. *(Paisley Museum)*

Young men and women taking part in activities provided by the YMCA. This photograph seems to have been taken in the 1970s to judge by the hairstyles. Are these people still as fit? Whatever they do now, they must have pleasant memories of their youth. *(Paisley YMCA)*

Judo at the YMCA. This is a much younger group of children, but look at the concentration on their faces! Here they take their judo seriously. This is still a popular activity at the YMCA and some participants reach a very high standard on completion of the course. *(Paisley YMCA)*

Players at St James's
bowling club, 1930. The
club won the *Daily
Record* trophy and had
also come top of the
Paisley and District
League. The St James's
bowling club and the
greens are now gone.
When roads and
motorways were built,
the bowling club and the
tennis courts were
casualties of the
development, as was a
large part of St James
Park. The park still has
football pitches that are
regularly used, but a
great area of the land
originally set aside for
recreation has
disappeared, a victim of
the needs of modern life.
(Alan Bennion)

Young cubs of the 33rd Paisley (Gleniffer) pack, after winning the PDCS Football Winter League for the 1979/80 season. They look very pleased with themselves, showing their medals and flag. It must have been a hard-fought battle to win the trophy and no doubt their mums and dads were cheering them on. *(Di Adam)*

Young Hugh Goudie and friends working hard to win their game of football at St James Park, 1950s.
(*Morag Goudie*)

These model plane makers are totally absorbed in what they are doing and taking pride in their skills. They were enjoying yet another activity offered by the YMCA. Today's members still have a great range of activities to choose from.
(*Paisley YMCA*)

8

Paisley People

A young Paisley Buddy concentrating on his music, late 1950s. Some children enjoy learning, others don't. Piano lessons are either great or ghastly, usually depending on your ability or how good your teacher is! *(Alan Bennion)*

The men of the Seedhill Home Guard, *c.* 1942. This was one of many Home Guard in Paisley, part of what became known as 'Dad's Army'. Many of these men were exempt from army service thanks to their 'reserved' occupations, which were vital to the war effort. They also did a great deal for the war in their spare time; many of them, after a hard day's work, would go straight to fire watching, first-aid posts or, of course, Home Guard duties. *(OPS)*

Mrs Ann Bennion posing in her back garden at 21 Argyle Street, 1950s. By this time taking pictures was not just the preserve of professional photographers, and this one was taken by Mr Bennion. *(Alan Bennion)*

Margaret Mitchell sitting with her grandson Edward in her garden at Oakshaw Street, 1930s. Note the greenhouse in the garden. Other tenants shared the garden and used the drying green for their clothes, but they would also have their own piece of ground for growing flowers and vegetables. *(Edward Farmer)*

A view of Oakshaw Street showing Coats Observatory and the former manse for Orr Square Church. The Observatory was one of the many gifts given by the Coats Thread family to the town. It is a wonderful building inside and out, and is now owned by Renfrewshire Council. It is still in operation and is well worth a visit. *(Edward Farmer)*

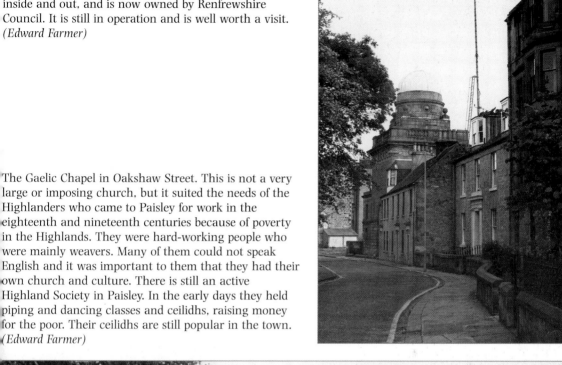

The Gaelic Chapel in Oakshaw Street. This is not a very large or imposing church, but it suited the needs of the Highlanders who came to Paisley for work in the eighteenth and nineteenth centuries because of poverty in the Highlands. They were hard-working people who were mainly weavers. Many of them could not speak English and it was important to them that they had their own church and culture. There is still an active Highland Society in Paisley. In the early days they held piping and dancing classes and ceilidhs, raising money for the poor. Their ceilidhs are still popular in the town. *(Edward Farmer)*

This picture was taken at a school camp in Aberfoyle, a regular destination for school trips in the 1940s and 1950s. The aim was to give children a chance to enjoy a stay in the countryside, as Paisley was a very industrial town then, and smog was a common problem. Parents would contribute to the cost of giving their children an extra holiday. *(Ann Wilson)*

Some of the young choristers of Paisley Abbey, 1983. They look like angels, but are they? Paisley Abbey choir is one of the best in the country and is much in demand. It has made several recordings in the past – once with Paisley's famous son, Kenneth McKellar – and will surely do so again in the future. *(Di Adam)*

The 9th Paisley Boy Scouts, who were based at the former Congregational Church in School Wind, 1958. Like many of the churches in Paisley this one was also sold off for housing. The boys sit proud and straight for their picture, dressed in their distinctive uniforms. Surely they cannot be wearing trainers? Are they old-style 'sandshoes'? *(Bruce Lindsay)*

Six of the boys from the 9th Scout Troup when they received their Queen Scout medals from District Commissioner Len Conquest in 1959. It was a wonderful honour for them, but they had to work hard to achieve it. *(Bruce Lindsay)*

The men of Thomas White & Son, a Paisley engineering company that was once a thriving business but has now gone. Like many other firms in the town, it made and repaired machinery for the huge textile mills, and when the mills went, so did White's. Most of the

country suffered the same fate as a result of modernisation and the need for fewer workers in this type of work. Engineering, textile and other industries either closed or moved abroad to places where the overheads were cheap. *(OPS)*

The piano tuners of Paisley, 1920s. At this time every family wanted to own a piano, and many did! To find a piano tuner now is quite a task, but, as one skill is no longer required, something else takes its place: now we all look for computer experts. *(Alex Imrie)*

Employees of Coats and Anchor Mills helping with the harvest at the annual harvest camp at Cockburnspath, near Dunbar, 1950. The mills gave permission for workers to go to these camps for a week each year, and two from each department were chosen. The purpose was to help farmers who were short of men and women to take in the harvest. The workers lived in dormitories of around twenty people. There was no mixing of the sexes in those days, and strict segregation was in force. The company made up the wages of anyone who volunteered to go. And a good time was had by all. *(Harry Hornby)*

A happy group of women from the Co-op shirt factory in Colinslee. The hairstyles and outfits in this picture suggest that it could only have been taken in the early 1960s. This was a works' outing and everyone is dressed in their best for the occasion. The factory was one of the Co-op's flagships for many years, but like many others it is now gone. *(Mima Pratt)*

One of the town's many amateur football clubs. This is the Smith's Crisps factory team. Many factories had their own teams, including Coats and Clarks, and each played in a different strip. The sides from the various companies competed for amateur trophies. There are still many amateur football teams in the town, but very few works' teams. *(Bruce Lindsay)*

A retirement party for Mary Spence, the lady sitting fourth from the left, 1958. She had spent all her working days in the mill. This was quite a grand affair, held in one of Paisley's large restaurants. Her co-workers spent a great deal of time putting together a book for her, which they called 'This is Your Life'. All the departments she had worked in and the friends she had made contributed to the book. It was produced by hand and is now on show in the Paisley Thread Mill Museum. *(Paisley Thread Mill Museum)*

A nostalgic picture taken in 1934 in Bank Street. Photographers would go around the streets where children were out playing, round up as many they could, take a picture and sell the image to the parents. Lots of money earned from one picture! *(Agnes McLean)*

Nineteen years later here are the 'Chums' of 1953, and a happy bunch they look! If a photographer tried the same today he would find the streets empty of children and probably be arrested too. However, many of these pictures will be treasured for the memories they stir in younger generations. *(Ricardo Napolatino)*

Another group of happy children, this time outside Mossvale School. The photographer managed to gather around twenty-one children for this picture. In the days when not every family had its own camera, this would have been one of the few images parents had of their children, which is why so many photographs like this have survived. *(Anne Wilson)*

Paisley and District Ladies Circle, the women's section of the Round Table, outside the former La Scala picture house at Hallowe'en 1971. These ladies were excellent fundraisers for charity, which is what they are doing here. They even dressed up for the occasion, with cloaks and witches' hats. The circle has now diminished as more women follow full-time careers. The La Scala cinema has of course now gone. *(Di Adam)*

Paisley thread mill workers in Asia. Seven of the men sitting in the second row were finishing-mill staff from Paisley who were just about to leave to return home, their women colleagues having already gone back to Scotland. Many thread mill workers travelled abroad to teach others how to operate mill machinery. Many countries had a tariff barrier to protect their

workforce and reduce their imports, so it was thought practical and profitable for Coats and Clarks to open branches abroad. It also gave Paisley workers the opportunity to travel and live in other parts of the world. The date of the picture is not recorded and the Old Paisley Society would welcome further information about it. *(OPS)*

A John Neilston School
sports day in the grounds of
Ferguslie Cricket Club. This
picture was taken in the late
1950s or early 1960s. This
school is now closed.
Fortunately the beautiful
building has been reused as
luxury flats. (*Alan Bennion*)

Pupils of the John Neilston School. A photograph with a famous face: in the second row from the top, fourth from the left, is well-known singer Kenneth McKellar. This school photograph will be in many a family's album. *(OPS)*

A later picture of the same school's pupils beautifully turned out for a class photograph in the 1950s. It is rather unfortunate that the trend is now for individual photographs instead of a class group. *(Alan Bennion)*

The class of 1910, Craigielea School. Built close to the Coats estate, the school benefited from a piece of land given to it by the family as an extra playground. The family presented prizes to pupils at the end of the summer term and the Old Paisley Society has in its collection a gold medal presented to a pupil. Unfortunately, this old school was burned down in the 1980s. *(OPS)*

The new Craigielea school, renamed St Fergus Primary, 1948. This school was built by Paisley Burgh at the same time as the Ferguslie Park housing scheme, and the children pictured here all lived in Ferguslie Park. By the 1930s the Coats family had moved and their estate was used mainly for housing, although a large part of it became a public park for the recreation of the townspeople, a function it still fulfils today. *(Eleanor McAlpine)*

Above: Camphill Senior Secondary School. Along with Paisley Grammar, John Neilston School, St Mirrin's Academy and St Margaret's Convent School, Camphill took children who had done well at primary school. Paisley Grammar, the John Neilston and St Margaret's were mainly fee-paying, so access to places there was limited. All these were the schools to which children aspired. The Camphill School has since been replaced, as have many of the others, and all schools in Paisley are now comprehensive. *(Paisley Museum)*

Opposite above: West School pupils, *c.* 1950. When education became compulsory, four schools were built in Paisley and were named North, South, East and West. Of course many more were built as the years went by and the population grew. *(Allan Bennion)*

Opposite below: Abercorn School, *c.* 1945. The school was built to serve pupils who moved into a new housing estate constructed by Paisley Burgh for families who had been living in tenement properties. The new estate gave people a much better standard of living – houses with bathrooms, hot water and, of course, gardens. *(Edward Farmer)*

Throughout this book there has been mention of Paisley's thread mills. For over 150 years they were the principal source of employment in the town. At one time there were over 10,000 people working in them and three times as many people working in firms that supplied them. Like many industrial towns across Britain, Paisley has suffered economically from the mills' demise and, indeed, demolition. However, a new use has been found for this particular building, as housing and business units. Its refurbishment involves many agencies, including the Phoenix Trust, Safeway, Renfrewshire Council and Scottish Enterprise (Renfrewshire). Standing in the foreground is Rena Shaw, a former mill girl aged a young 94. How fitting it was that Rena performed the honours at the ground-breaking ceremony in 2003. *(Rena Shaw)*

Author Evelyn Hood and her husband James with Paisley South MP Douglas Alexander at the launch of a book compiled and edited by Evelyn, 2003. Evelyn had spoken to many former mill workers about their days in the mills. The proceeds of this book are being donated to Paisley Thread Mill Museum, so that it can continue to tell generations to come the story of the mills and the people who worked in them. *(OPS)*

Ann Bennion pushing baby Alan down the High Street in the 1950s. *(Alan Bennion)*

ACKNOWLEDGEMENTS

Thank you to the many people who provided photographs for this book and to the people who allowed us to copy precious family pictures.

Thanks also to Sadie Turnbull for her help in reproducing photographs. Any images not acknowledged are from the Old Paisley Society archives.

A special thanks to Old Paisley Society Secretary Hazel Lindsay and Vice-President Di Adam. This book could not have been compiled without their help.

Ellen Farmer MBE